MIRABE

a story told by Chris Goode

OBERON BOOKS
LONDON

WWW.OBERONBOOKS.COM

First published in 2018 by Oberon Books Ltd
521 Caledonian Road, London N7 9RH
Tel: +44 (0) 20 7607 3637 / Fax: +44 (0) 20 7607 3629
e-mail: info@oberonbooks.com
www.oberonbooks.com

A catalogue record for this book is available from the British Library.

PB ISBN: 9781786827005
E ISBN: 9781786826992

Cover design: Dragonfly

Printed and bound by 4EDGE Limited, Hockley, Essex, UK.
eBook conversion by Lapiz Digital Services, India.

10 9 8 7 6 5 4 3 2 1

Mirabel was first performed at Ovalhouse, London, on 31 October 2018.

The company was as follows:

Writer / Performer	**Chris Goode**
Director	**Rebecca McCutcheon**
Set and Costume Designer	**Naomi Dawson**
Lighting Designer	**Lee Curran**
Sound Designer	**Matt Padden**
Animation	**Lou Sumray**
Technical Stage Manager	**Ciara Shrager**
Production Manager	**Helen Mugridge**

Lee Curran Lighting Designer

Theatre includes: *Jesus Christ Superstar, As You Like It* (Regent's Park); *Summer and Smoke, Dance Nation* (Almeida); *Constellations, Gundog, Road, Nuclear War, A Profoundly Affectionate, Passionate Devotion to Someone (-Noun); X, Linda* (Royal Court); *Jubilee* (Royal Exchange/Lyric Hammersmith); *The Lady From The Sea, Splendour* (Donmar); *Hamlet, Blindsided* (Royal Exchange); *Woyzeck* (Birmingham Rep); *A Streetcar Named Desire, The Weir* (ETT/Touring); *Black Men Walking* (Eclipse/touring); *Cover My Tracks* (Old Vic); *Doctor Faustus* (RSC); *The Winter's Tale* (Lyceum, Edinburgh); *Imogen* (Globe); *Depart, Turfed* (LIFT); *Kissing The Shotgun Goodnight* (Christopher Brett Bailey); *A Number* (Young Vic/Nuffield); *Mametz* (NT Wales); *Protest Song* (NT).

Dance and opera include: *Blak Whyte Gray* (Boy Blue); *Rosalind, Within Her Eyes* (James Cousins); *Sun, Political Mother, In Your Rooms, The Art Of Not Looking Back, Uprising* (Hofesh Shechter); *Untouchable* (Royal Ballet); *Clowns* (NDT); *Tomorrow, Frames, Curious Conscience* (Rambert); *Orphee Et Eurydice* (ROH); *Tosca* (Opera North).

Naomi Dawson Set and Costume Designer

Naomi trained at Wimbledon School of Art and Kunstacademie, Maastricht.

Recent theatre design includes: with Chris Goode: *Every One* (BAC); *Weaklings* (Warwick Arts and UK Tour); *Men in the Cities* (Royal Court/Traverse Theatre and UK tour); *Landscape and Monologue* (Ustinov, Bath); *King Pelican* (Drum Theatre, Plymouth). With others: *The Woods* (Royal Court); *As You Like It* (Regents Park); *Happy Days* (Royal Exchange); *The Duchess of Malfi, Doctor Faustus, The White Devil, The Roaring Girl, King John, As You Like It* (RSC); *Much Ado About Nothing* (Rose Theatre Kingston); *Tin Drum* (Kneehigh/Liverpool Everyman); *The Winter's Tale* (Romateatern, Gotland); *Beryl* (West Yorkshire Playhouse and UK tour); *Kasimir and Karoline, Fanny and Alexander* (Malmo Stadsteater); *Brave New World* (Northampton and UK Tour); *Hotel, Three More Sleepless Nights* (National Theatre); *Wildefire, Belongings* (Hampstead Theatre); *Dancing at Lughnasa* (Theatre Royal, Northampton); *Amerika, Krieg der Bilder* (Staatstheater Mainz); *Mary Shelley, The Glass Menagerie* (Shared Experience); *State of Emergency, Mariana Pineda* (Gate Theatre); *The Container* (Young Vic).

Opera designs include: *Madama Butterfly* (Grimeborn, Arcola); *The Lottery, The Fairy Queen* (Bury Court Opera).

Chris Goode Writer/Performer

Chris Goode is a writer, director and maker for theatre and live performance. A former artistic director of Camden People's Theatre, he now leads Chris Goode & Company, which he established in 2011 with producer Ric Watts and critical writer Maddy Costa. Recent work includes: for CG&Co: *Jubilee* (Royal Exchange / Lyric Hammersmith); *Wanted* (Transform '16 at West Yorkshire Playhouse); *Every One* (BAC); *Weaklings* (Warwick Arts Centre); *Men in the Cities* (Traverse / Royal Court); *STAND* (Oxford Playhouse); *Monkey Bars* (Unicorn / Traverse); *GOD/HEAD* (Ovalhouse); *The Adventures of Wound Man and Shirley* (BAC). Outside the company: *User Not Found* (for Dante or Die); *EVE* (with Jo Clifford for National Theatre of Scotland); *What If I Told You?* (Mayers Ensemble); *Mad Man* (Drum, Plymouth); *The Worst of Scottee* (Roundhouse); *Who You Are* (Tate Modern); …*SISTERS* (Gate / Headlong). In 2010 he joined the international touring cast of Tim Crouch's acclaimed *The Author*.

Chris is the recipient of four Scotsman Fringe First awards, as well as the inaugural The Stage Special Award in 2014. Since 2012 he has produced and presented the acclaimed theatre podcast Thompson's Live, and in 2015 Oberon Books published his first full-length critical book, *The Forest and the Field: Changing theatre in a changing world.*

Rebecca McCutcheon Director

Rebecca is a Peckham-based theatre director, working in site-based performance, new writing (Chris Goode, Philip Ridley) and devised performance (*Bette & Joan* for Foursight). She co-founded angels in the architecture (2000-2008). As well as her site-specific work, Rebecca has worked in roles with the National Theatre, the Almeida Theatre, the Gate Theatre and the RSC.

In 2017 Rebecca co-founded Lost Text/Found Space to create site-based work with unperformed female-authored plays. Her work with Lost Text/Found Space occupies a unique artistic space, creating performances aimed at kicking women's writing into the foreground. *Til We Meet in England* (2018) saw the company occupy Safehouse in Peckham.

Rebecca is Teaching Fellow in the Drama Department at Royal Holloway, University of London, and has published articles and chapters on her site-based research-practice.

For more info see www.RebeccaMcCutcheon.com and www.losttextfoundspace.com.

Helen Mugridge Production Manager

Helen is an experienced stage and production manager. Her previous credits include: *Placebo* (Clod Ensemble); *I'm a Phoenix, Bitch* (Bryony Kimmings at BAC); *Are You Deaf Yet?* (Christopher Brett Bailey triple bill, BAC); *Almost Always Muddy, Likely Story* (Kirsty Harris); *Oranges and Elephants* (Lil Warren and Susie McKenna, Hoxton Hall); *The Shape of the Pain* (Rachel Bagshaw and Chris Thorpe with China Plate); *Getting Dressed* (Secondhanddance, UK tour); *Manpower* (Two Destination Language, UK tour); *Kissing the Shotgun Goodnight* (Christopher Brett Bailey, UK tour); *Sleepless* and *Stowaway* (Analogue); *Golem* (1927).

Matt Padden Sound Designer

Matt was the National Theatre of Scotland's Head of Sound between 2008 and 2017. His designs for that company include: *Eve, How To Act, Last Tango in Partick, Last Dream (On Earth)* (presented by Kai Fischer); *The Tin Forest, A Christmas Carol, Long Gone Lonesome, Wall of Death – A Way of Life* and, as Technical Sound Designer, *Enquirer.*

Other recent designs include *The 306:Dusk* (NTS/Perth Theatre); *Mancub* (Cumbernauld Theatre); *The Three Musketeers* (Dukes Lancaster); *Long Day's Journey Into Night* (Citizens Theatre); *The Hidden* (Visible Fictions); *What Put The Blood* (Abbey Theatre Dublin); *Cockpit* (Royal Lyceum Theatre Edinburgh); *Heroine* (MJW Productions); *Expensive Shit* (Scottish Theatre Producers); *Shrapnel* (Theatre Gu Leòr); *Andromaque* (Òran Mór); *Entartet* (Kai Fischer); *Subway* (Vanishing Point) and *Woyzeck* (Corcadorca Theatre Company).

Ciara Shrager Technical Stage Manager

Ciara is a freelance lighting designer and technical stage manager. Most recently, she has worked with ThisEgg as a relighter and operator on their tour of award-winning family show, *Me and My Bee*, and she worked as a venue technician for Underbelly for the duration of the Edinburgh Fringe Festival in 2018. She is an associate artist of multi-award winning theatre company Emergency Chorus, and was the lighting designer and technical manager on the tour of their debut show *CELEBRATION* in the summer of 2017. Her favourite things to work on involve collaborative, experimental art forms that lets her be as playful as those on stage.

Lou Sumray Animator

Brought up in the south, living in the north and absorbed in drawing, which has recently included animation, Lou's first involvement with Chris Goode & Co was as an artist-in-residence documenting rehearsals for *9* at West Yorkshire Playhouse in 2012, where her iPad drawings became animated for the show. For the Transform '16 festival Lou went on to create a three-minute animation for CG&Co's *Wanted*. As a member of 154collective, a multi art form group, Lou drew her first (award-winning) stop motion piece 'Follow me' for the show *Under The Bed*.

She writes: 'I love charcoal, the directness of it, but drawing on an iPad brings something else, it's obviously digital but I am drawing with my finger.'

for Griffyn

and in loving memory of
Charlie 'Tornado' Kane

the night belongs to you

"You've got to put your bodies upon the gears and upon the wheels, upon the levers, upon all the apparatus, and you've got to make it stop, and you've got to indicate to the people who run it, to the people who own it, that unless you are free, the machine will be prevented from working at all."

—Mario Savio, December 1964

If I was crying
In the van with my friend
It was for freedom
From myself and from the land

I made a lot of mistakes

—Sufjan Stevens, from 'Chicago'

Zero.

An expanse of soft music, while everyone's coming in. Then, quiet.

CHRIS, the teller of the story, steps out in front of the audience. He is smartly dressed in a dark suit with a white shirt; no tie.

He takes some time to look at everyone, before he speaks.

Hello.

I want to tell you a story about a little girl called Mirabel.

I think you already know that the title of the story is also *Mirabel*.

Not everybody has the same name as the story they're in.

So that should tell you something about Mirabel.

This isn't a true story, yet.

But by the time I've finished telling it, who knows.

Some stories, you have no idea where or when or how they begin.

Others, you know exactly.

The gentlest music.

CHRIS takes off his jacket and hangs it up; unbuttons and rolls up the sleeves of his smart white shirt. And then he starts to tell the story.

* * *

It was a boy in Mirabel's class at school who was the first one to die.

A redheaded, redfaced boy called Henry with sticky-out ears and a doughnut in his pocket for later.

He was the first to see it coming out of a clear blue nowhere, and then he was the first to die.

There was an impossibly loud commotion which he could not hear, because he already belonged to a silence.

The silence came up to Henry and hugged him tight and Henry promised the silence that he wouldn't cry.

His mum and dad watched him die. And then they watched each other die.

A girl called Prudence on her paper round died. Just bicycled into the unexpected shortcut of her own disappearance.

Ronnie Barker the chocolate labrador from down the road died in a vortex of ineffable happiness, chasing his own tail as he loved to do, until it finally vanished, and the rest of him followed on behind.

The local cub scouts watched Akela turn to an electrical storm of atoms, and then to the calm after the storm. "Akela!" they shouted. "We'll do our best!" And then they died too, all in a row.

Worms and maggots and spiders died, and chickens and peacocks. Deep in the forests of Gabon, a gorilla died. And then all the gorillas died.

On their first day in their new jobs and on the day of their retirement and on every day between, all of the firefighters died. All of the acrobats. All of the pigs and butterflies and every king and queen.

All the yaks and the caribou ran into the ocean to try to escape their fate. And then the ocean died with them inside it.

Popular numbers like 14 and 23 and 1006 collapsed and gave up their factors to the terrible whirlwinds; and all the lonely soldiers died, far from home, standing on their heads inside their appointed softboiled eggs.

All but a dozen of the world's crows were liquidized into a vast black haunted smoothie and sucked like a reverse scream into the great mouth of the insatiable sky.

The corals saw the writing on the wall and multitudinously took their own lives.

Paul McCartney died live on television in Japan but there was hardly anyone left to see him go, and in twenty more seconds, there was no one on earth who knew his name or remembered a single one of his songs except Ob-La-Di Ob-La-Da, which lived on in the mind of a caged cockatoo in a suburb of Amsterdam as it slowly starved to death.

The buttercups died, and the Galapagos turtles: and all the radio telescopes frantically searching for intelligent life anywhere in the universe went dead at the same time.

Every eel and every emu, every shark and every human grandmother, of every degree of kindness.

And almost every known hunger or affection ended, almost every recrimination and inquiry and almost every instinct for survival. And every pencil fell to the floor.

Now picture with me for a moment your worst enemy and your best friend, because they were in this story for a second or two, and then they died; and all those who counted you as their best friend or their worst enemy died with the spectre of you in their minds. All of them gone in a half heartbeat.

The person sitting next to you this evening died.

And then you died.

The story of Mirabel began eight years before the end of the world.

But we're going to skip those first eight years, aren't we?

We know how this actually starts.

The incredible violent cacophony of the end of the world.

It's unbearable and it goes on and on.

And then, quite suddenly, it stops. And on we go.

One.

Not quite silence, but space.

CHRIS has changed into the storyteller's outfit. There's something kind of alien about it. It's his job to be somebody else for a while.

The morning after the world before.

Mirabel, after the end of the end of the world, is not alone.

A little beetle potters across her face. And this is how we know she is not dead.

Whole cathedrals have fallen out of the sky and smashed in her back garden: but it takes the tiny sockless feet of a green-black beetle to bring Mirabel round.

Come back to us, love.

Her eyelids tremble, and her lips part just enough for a timid vowel to come out, see the day, and go back in again.

The beetle pauses for a moment. Thinks something sad about mathematics. You'd be surprised how often that happens to a beetle.

It's so quiet you can hear the no-longer-ticking of all the vanquished clocks.

After the beetle's feet, it's the silence that wakes Mirabel.

And then the deceitful silence reveals itself, takes off its disguise and slowly slowly reveals itself as the most impossible pain.

First it's like the chorus of an out-of-tune song going round and round in her foot. And then she notices toothache. Jaw. Ear.

Nest of bees. Glass and agony. Something's making her body throw the pain like a ventriloquist throws their voice. Bad sort of mouth gaping where the first fire happened. Elongated weather conditions. Blackbird of pain, singing on a distant windowledge, a sadness to save for later.

Whole room's dizzy. Come on, room. Lie down. Close your eyes now.

Mirabel wants to call for her dad.

She's supposed to want to call for her mum but she wants to call for her dad.

This is not ordinary pain that needs kissing and holding and soothing and sort of cherishing, sort of welcoming in.

This is the kind of pain that rips the whole sky from throat to abdomen and hundreds and thousands of original pirate cutlasses fall out.

This can only be fixed by someone who never cries. Who doesn't have a favourite colour or a favourite animal.

She wants to call for her dad.

But that's not the sound that comes, when it comes. Because she deeply knows her mum and dad are dead. Or that somehow anyway the idea of them is dead, that it died inside her as she slept, amid the bruises that bloomed inside her skeleton.

So the sound that comes is not Mum, or Dad.

Bear, she says.

Bear.

The beetle runs away and hides behind a Disney's *Frozen* snowglobe that Mirabel will never ever think about again.

Bear, she says.

Mirabel, says Bear.

You're here! she says.

I'm always here, says Bear.

And now she can feel his hand in hers and she squeezes it so tight that in another kind of story, it would bring tears to Bear's remaining eye—his lone glass eye, Mirabel having gouged out the other one with a spoon and spat it out the window into the neighbours' garden because she so badly needed to know what it felt like to do specifically that.

That's right, says Bear. You can squeeze me.

You can squeeze me back, says Mirabel, and he does, just a little, just to humour her.

They squeeze their way into a passage of time through the dry clockless silence of the lying-down bedroom and the last souvenirs.

Bear looks around, in so far as he can. He looks at Mirabel. She looks like just debris.

Bloody mess, says Bear.

And Mirabel's heart squeezes itself for gladness as she remembers being sent to her bedroom for saying 'bloody', and how she held Bear tight and point blank refused to cry and whispered into Bear's ear: bloody, bloody, bloody, bloody... All night long. Bloody, bloody. Till she fell asleep, and he faithfully dreamed her voice on her behalf, I'll carry you, bloody, bloody, bloody, until he too fell asleep.

Bloody mess, agrees Mirabel, only now she understands that this is a description of her.

Well then, she thinks.

And in an instant she forgets her favourite colour.

And she forgets her favourite animal.

And she'll never cry again.

Don't go back to sleep now, says Bear. It's dangerous.

I won't, she says, and instantly she does.

And for a second or two she's a very long way away. Waving back from the far shore.

But she's still right here. So it can't be her.

* * *

There's a stone dead owl at Mirabel's feet, but that's not why she's stopped.

There are wires all over the earth, either fallen wires or wires that have come to the surface. Lonely plastics in all the bright colours of alien fruit. A kid's pedal car, flat as a rug now, and an upright piano on its side, like a dog that's been bullied into learning to beg. A backyard trampoline turned black and partly melted and no backyard anyway. Or it's all become infinite backyard now.

I say this with all respect, says Bear to Mirabel. Do we have a plan? … It's all right if we don't.

Mirabel's lost in thought.

She has a satchel on a shoulderstrap, thinks Bear, that's the next best thing to a plan.

8

The satchel contains: a school exercise book, hardly used, and a purple felt-tip pen that smells like robot blueberries; a royal blue school sweater with a motif of a dragonfly; a descant recorder, with cleaning rod and go-faster stripes; an exceedingly sharp pink-handled kitchen knife; an unopened three-tube multipack of Chewits, which for all we know are the only edible foodstuff in the world to have survived the apocalypse; a pack of Disney's *Frozen* sticking plasters which suddenly reveals itself to have been not such a rubbish Christmas stocking present after all; and a half-full disposable camera that she kept from her mum and dad's wedding reception the summer before last.

There's our plan, thinks Bear. It's in there somewhere.

She hasn't just brought a load of random shit.

Our plan is, says Mirabel, we're going to find a grown-up.

That's what I was told to do. By people I trust.

In an emergency, tell a grown-up.

Tell them what?, says Bear.

Just tell them, says Mirabel.

So many things are missing, all around, or they've become soot or powder, or scrunched up balls of burnished metal, or unhinged silhouettes.

There's a strange orange glow to everything, a new variety of radiation.

Mirabel can't say any of her fear out loud so it's making her tongue go dry instead, and the roof of her mouth, and her lips. She's going to have to not pay attention to that. There's lots of things we can be now in this stub of a world, but thirsty isn't one of them.

The distance in every direction feels so impossible.

The trees are all stand-up corpses. Spent matchsticks struck against the rough dead skin of the sky.

Where do you think all the grown-ups are? he says.

Mirabel and Bear together, still and strange as two wading storks in a museum display case.

A bumblebee comes into their orbit. Sound first, then body. It's bleached quite white by whatever the thing was that did that. We're going to need new words for everything, thinks Mirabel. She adds it to her mental list of things we're going to need.

They'll all have gone to a grown-up place for a pow-wow, says Mirabel. For a stock-take.

They'll all have met up at the garden centre or something stupid.

She can't say, and Bear can't say, what they saw in the corner of their eyes and eye respectively, when she climbed down the remains of the bannisters to get the kitchen knife from what used to be the kitchen drawer.

Dad, quite the wrong shape of dad, and all smudgy and red.

Mum, lying impossibly across him, impersonating all the wrong angles. Legs bent the wrong way at the knees.

Mirabel convulses silently inside herself.

Come along then, says Bear. Which way's the garden centre?

The colour seems to be draining out of the sky.

Bear hangs from Mirabel's hand.

The garden centre is not that far, she's thinking. Unless it's not there.

Two.

Time drags its wounded body along the ground to keep pace with Mirabel and Bear.

Day bleeds out, leaving fractured night to its own lonely devices.

It takes till the lowest minor chords of twilight to reach the place that was possibly the site of the garden centre.

Nothing remains but a heap of twisted secateurs and a potted cactus that looks like a bum.

I expect all the adults finished early and went to the pub, says Mirabel.

Kindly armageddon has spattered the earth with campfires. That's one thing they don't have to build tonight.

They choose one and Mirabel sits on the ground, on her folded blue sweater. Bear sits on Mirabel's lap for a bit, but it's not comfy, and in the end they agree he'll sit beside her instead. He sits on a friendly-looking rock, about the size of an adult's decapitated head.

It occurs to Mirabel for the first time that she doesn't have to do her homework, and just for a moment she misses it so hard, like it's a lost photo of someone who died.

Bear is doing vigilance.

I saw red, he suddenly says. I saw bright red.

The campfire is quiet. The universe is quiet.

Red red red red red, says Bear. And then he says: Look.

11

At the far threshold of the light of the fire stands a dog. A sleek, stark, unafraid black dog with bright red laserbeam eyes.

Doggie, says Mirabel. Come here dog. Come on.

He's not our dog, says Bear. I don't think he's anyone's dog. Let's let him be.

But the dog walks over and stands in front of Mirabel. Black and red and never less unafraid.

Mirabel, says Mirabel, and she holds out her hand to the dog.

The dog looks at Mirabel's hand in a way that Bear can see that the dog knows Mirabel's hand is made out of basically dog food.

Good dog, says Mirabel. Shake hands.

Girl, says the dog. Nothing about me is good.

* * *

By the deep orange light of the shuddering fire, Mirabel holds in her small careful hand the dogtag that the dog wears around his neck. She can't make out what it says.

URBAN, says the dog. It's my name.

That's a funny name, she says, not unkindly.

Look though, says Urban. It's only half a tag. It's only the left half of a broken nametag.

I go by Urban, says Urban, but it's not the whole of my name. My name is Urban Warrior.

Fancy, says Bear very quietly to himself.

12

Let me remind you I'm a dog, says Urban. I can hear the things you say to yourself. Sometimes I can hear what you're thinking.

Bear tries not to think what he's already thinking.

What does Urban Worrier mean, asks Mirabel?

Warrior, says Urban. Not Worrier. Warrior. It means I come from the streets. The streets are mine. When the time comes I'll die on the streets, with pride.

What streets?, thinks Bear.

It means I'll bite your fucking arm, says Urban.

Mirabel unwraps another Chewit. You can choose what flavour.

Bear isn't really called Bear, she says. Are you, Bear?

Bear looks up. Something in his chest feels tight.

I got him when I was three, says Mirabel. He was a Christmas present from my grandma when I was three. Not my nice grandma. My thin grandma.

She said: He's come to stay with you and his name is Mister Wiggle-Ears Fudgebear Esquire. She's like, Can you say that?

I'm like, Of course I can say it, I choose not to, it's incredibly stupid.

I didn't say that to her. I said, I'm just going to call him Bear please. Because he's a bear.

She gave me cash for Christmas every year after that.

I don't care, says Mirabel. Bear's just Bear. Aren't you, Bear?

Bear has a sudden strange daydream. He's remembering fire engines in the distance, and ambulances. Not for the end of the world, but in the time before. And how he longed somehow to hug tight to himself the sound of emergency sirens in the distance. How he longed to fall asleep sometimes holding that sound.

No, says Bear. Since you ask.

Urban looks at Bear, and lies down.

Don't be silly, Bear, says Mirabel.

Over their heads, the black sky is stretched almost to tearing point. From time to time they can hear one pipistrelle, one nightjar. Never more than one of anything. The world's become a reverse Noah's Ark. One of everything, for dying out.

Before you ever held me, Mirabel, says Bear, the sensation I knew best in myself was the texture of the forest floor. I knew I looked to the world like plush, like high-street plush, but the taste I knew best was the iron hit of a slaughtered badger or rat.

I know the smell of my own sweat and I know how to call across tremendous distance.

I know the mystery of hackles, and I know the chase.

My name is not Bear, says Bear.

My name is Wolf.

It's hardly perceptible, but Urban lowers his head.

Say Wolf, says Wolf to Mirabel.

Mirabel says nothing. She picks up Wolf from his rock and puts him in her lap and holds him to her chest.

Wolf, says Urban, like it's Amen.

Mirabel wishes she knew the time. But it doesn't really matter any more. The time is profound night.

Urban Warrior, says Urban, means I'll come along with you, as far as you want me to come. And on the way I'll stand between you and any harm.

Two individual tears come to Mirabel's tired eyes, and drool down her cheeks. She feels her bottom lip start to go and she checks herself, because the story says she'll never cry again: so she can't—at least not in front of you.

Looking around for a joke to console herself, she reaches out a hand to the rock that sits beside them. She pets it on its smooth upper surface.

And what's *your* real name, little rock? she says.

Baheegwing, says the rock—whose name, it turns out, since she asked, is Baheegwing.

* * *

It's the same, over and over. What starts as a faraway dot takes shape, in the rhythm of their trudging; slowly gradually becomes a form, and then a thing, and then a thing that can be named, and finally a landmark.

A shit-green statue of a bisected general or an old prime minister with his head stoved in.

A red bus sleeping on its side, all smashed up and scrawled with obscene falsehoods.

It's always Urban who sees them first; then Mirabel; then Wolf, but he can't judge depth of field.

Once they're a landmark, they're a target.

Landmark 17. 18.

Landmark 19 is the smallest so far.

It's a park bench, in good order, and an old cast-iron lamppost standing over it. The only elements for miles around that look like what they're supposed to look like.

Mirabel counts down the footsteps between her and the bench.

Her lip is quivering again: now with exertion. This heaviness. As they come to the bench, Mirabel almost falls. She jettisons her satchel.

It's too much heavy, she says.

I wonder, says Wolf, if it was altogether wise to bring the rock.

Baheegwing, says Baheegwing, as Mirabel places him gently down on the seat.

Well he wanted to come, says Mirabel. It's hardly fair to leave him behind just because he can't do his own walking.

Once you're in the gang, you're in the gang, says Mirabel. Plus, he's not that heavy. It's me that's heavy.

What else? says Urban. What else have you brought?

Mirabel, in the grand silence of the new desert, listens within herself for heavy objects.

What is it? says Urban.

My homework, she says. French vocab test.

Oh, she says. I don't need to know French any more.

There's nobody left to speak it with.

That's right, says Urban. Dead language now.

Mirabel listens to the French swarming inside her. It will have to be released into the wild. It must have its freedom.

Mirabel climbs onto the bench seat and looks out at where the vast ground gives way to the immense sky. And in the sky she finds everything that's familiar to her. The streaks of known colour and the calm secrecies. The motion of thin air. The memory of a balloon festival in a far off city that's extinct.

Her dry tongue across her dry lips.

She wonders if this will hurt. Everything will hurt from now on, she thinks. Why not this?

She takes an ordinary breath, and begins.

Le chien.

Le chat. Le cheval. La chauve-souris. Le chien.

Le chien. Le loup.

Le lion. Le tigre. Le loup. Le lapin. Le hamster. Le ver. Le virus.

Maman. Papa. L'ours. No. Le loup. Le secret. Non, je suis fille unique.

Nous vivons ensemble. No. Non. Tout le monde est parti.

Je suis heureuse. Je suis triste. Le garçon est méchant. Les enfants sont malheureux. Pourquoi est-ce tu es triste? Pourquoi est-ce tu es fâché? Pourquoi est-ce tu es furieux? Je suis désolé. Nous sommes désolés.

Le chien. Ouaf! Ouaf! Le chien. Le chêvre. Bêê! Le ver. Le loup. Le roche. L'âne brait. Hi han!

La tête. Le visage. Le front. La gorge. J'ai un chat dans la gorge.
[Laugh.]

J'ai faim.

J'ai faim. J'ai soif. Je suis malade. Je suis fatiguée. J'ai peur. J'ai
mal ici. J'ai mal à la tête. J'ai de la fièvre. J'ai mal à l'oreille. J'ai le
mal des transports. Je suis brûlée par le soleil. J'ai le vertige. Au
secours! Bon anniversaire!

Le doigt. Le pouce. La bouche. La gorge. La cage thoracique. Le
coeur. Le poumon. Le foie. Le feu. Les feux d'artifice. J'ai mal
aux feux d'artifice. Pourquoi tu me déteste?

Le chien. Ouaf! Ouaf! Le loup. Ooouh! La roche. Baheegwing!
Le lion. Raoh! Les abeilles. Bzzzz. Toutes les abeilles. BZZZZZ!
Le miel, la confiture, la marmelade. Beaucoup de marmelade!
Oeufs brouillé. L'ovule. Le sperme. J'ai mal au vagin. Jean
Valjean. Je dors si mal. Je rêve toujours des ovnis.

Soudainement. Souvent. Rarement. Presque rien. Quelquefois.
De temps en temps. De jour en jour. Néanmoins elle a persisté.
Aujourd'hui. Hier. Autrefois. Les disparus. Les morts. Les fantômes.
Hou!

La blancheur. La atrocité. Les astéroïdes. Les dinosaures.
Urgence! Le virus. Le ver. La vérité. La vie en rose.

Le secret du chien. Le secret de la roche. La fleur à venir. L'avion
blessé.

L'avion blessé.

The wounded aeroplane.

There, in the distance, from the vantage of the park bench,
Mirabel sees that Landmark 20 will be a wounded plane.

Three.

It's as if a vast multicoloured dream has coughed up a lump
of tangled metal, and it's landed here to be a landmark, this
complicated heap of screwball wasteland garbage.

The quiet air ripples with the heat that ascends from the crumpled
fuselage of the light aircraft.

Mirabel and Wolf, and Urban and Baheegwing, stand dumbly by,
like redundant shepherds at a stillborn nativity.

The pilot hangs out of what's left of the cockpit like the tongue
hangs out of a stupid dog's mouth on a hot afternoon. He's just
lolling there.

His face is so intricately bloody that it's easy to assume, it's hard
not to, that he's dead.

But to an eight-year-old girl on a quest to find a grown-up,
watching a man's face with superhuman attention, the merest
flicker of an eyelid is itself as voluptuously big as a plane crash in
the desert.

She walks up to the pilot and stands over him.

Hello, she says. I'm Mirabel and these are my friends.

We need your assistance as soon as you can wake up, please, she says.

Mayday mayday mayday.

No part of the pilot is flickering now, unless it's deep inside.

Just out of reach of the near side wing tip, a bluebell bends slightly
to adapt to a gentle gust of wind. Nobody sees.

Urban walks over and barks in the pilot's face.

Woh woh woh woh woh.

Mayday mayday mayday, says Mirabel, translating.

Wolf is tired and full of hurt. Baheegwing is—just is.

The bluebell waits her turn.

We should move on, says Urban. Look at the state of the aircraft. He never stood a chance.

It's down to us now, says Urban. The animals. This is a time for the resilience of animals.

Hello? says Mirabel. We need assistance. We are very very very extremely lost.

And deep inside the pilot, something flickers.

* * *

Night and the new campfire kissing each other lavishly as the pilot is speaking.

I'm not the sort of person who thinks this, says the pilot. But I saw the face of God. I swear I did. In the eye of that storm that brought me down. That was his eye. That strange tranquility.

A giddy insect climbs the north face of Baheegwing, like a hero.

The name's Darkling, says the pilot. Flying Officer Richard Darkling. Some of the chaps call me Duckling. You can call me Duckling. I don't mind.

Does anyone else's head hurt? says Duckling.

Mirabel looks at Woolf.

They pass Duckling's water canteen around the circle again. Mirabel drinks, and Urban. Wolf declines. Mirabel wets her finger and draws a smiley face on Baheegwing.

This may be a silly question in the circumstances, says Duckling, but what, actually, sort of assistance do you need? Do you know? You might not know.

We've been walking for three or four days I think, says Mirabel. We wanted to find a grown-up. To tell.

Ah! says Duckling. To tell what?

Just to tell, says Mirabel. We don't know what to say, exactly. We're just us.

No I know, says Duckling.

I wish I could help, he says, I do, but I don't honestly think I qualify.

My plane crashed in a terrible storm and I dreamt that I was dead. And I see that I'm not dead, but my head hurts very badly and my leg. And my lungs. And my feelings. And my aeroplane. And I've never really been that sort of grown-up, to be honest. The sort to be told the things.

Honestly I think I should be on your team, really.

Everyone looks at the fire. Tonight seems colder than last night.

Well then, says Mirabel. You should come with us. We'll just keep going until we find an actual grown-up.

My leg's really quite squiffy, though, says Duckling. And he's correct. His right leg is not really a leg now. It's a sort of tapering corkscrew of meat and gravy shimmering crimson red between shreds of trouser-leg.

I'm not confident I wouldn't go around in circles, he says.

Well, says Mirabel. Once you're in the gang you're in the gang.

Are you in the gang?

I'm not sure, says Duckling. But it's a very pleasant thought.

Well think about it while we sleep, says Mirabel. Tomorrow's a different day.

I think you're more grown-up than I bloody am, says Duckling.

* * *

The sky in every direction is the strange phantom colour of uncooked egg white. This is what passes for a different day now.

Duckling wakes up choking, and the image of the carcass of the world comes into focus. Mirabel is kneeling by the wounded aircraft, as if she's saying childish prayers. Wolf sits patiently next to her. Urban is nowhere to be seen.

Slowly, as though acting out a terrible grudge, the pilot manages to stand, waveringly, imitating a shape with no name and then, as he walks towards Mirabel, a rhythm with no numbers.

She's so beautiful, Mirabel is saying. She's perfect.

Mirabel cradles the tired head of the bluebell in her palm.

I wonder if she knows, says Mirabel.

Bluebell, says Duckling. Damnedest thing.

She's going to come with us, says Mirabel.

I'm not sure that's a good idea, says Duckling. I can't think she'll like the journey.

She's a survivor, says Mirabel—and it's hard to argue with that, surrounded as they are by the wide open space made by so many hundreds of thousands of perished things.

Suddenly Urban is sprinting out of the distance, with a long heavy stick clenched in his jaws. He lays the stick at Duckling's foot.

This is for you, says Urban. To help you walk.

Oh! says Duckling. Thank you for your kindness.

Thank you for your service, says Urban.

Duckling looks at him.

What on earth do you think I did? he says.

It's slow arduous work treading out the morning, slower by half now that Duckling's with them. Every few paces he has to stop and lean hard on his stick. It has to take not only his body weight, but the weight of his wretchedness too, and the weight of his secrets, and how he was a useless brother and a hopeless son.

Nor can it help to have Baheegwing under his arm. No one left behind, says Duckling, and Mirabel nods approvingly.

She's named the bluebell Salad. She says it's a pretty name but Urban understands. When you're very hungry, everything around you divides into food and not-food.

Mirabel carries Salad in one hand and Wolf hangs from the other. Urban has sprinted off into the beyond. Something has freaked him out today.

I've realised something, says Wolf to Mirabel, sneaking his voice in between the silences.

Does Urban smell like a stray dog to you?

What does a stray dog smell like?, Wolf you oddity, says Mirabel.

He smells like washed hands, says Wolf. He smells like a pillowcase that's never been slept on.

Mirabel shushes him. Urban is sprinting back towards them, his red eyes blaring.

Doggo! says Mirabel. We missed you!

Urban looks at them all, then at the ground, and then at Mirabel.

It's time to stop, miss, says Urban.

Time to go back home.

It's too much. It's too big.

You're only little.

We're all little.

Duckling's walking dead. The rock's dead anyway. Your flower's going to die.

You and Wolf should go back home and wait for the emergency grown-ups to find you.

Urban pauses. The complicated sound he can hear in the distance is of an adult lizard eating a baby lizard.

Urban you are silly, says Mirabel. There are no grown-ups.

Then what are we doing?, says Urban.

We're doing the thing you do, she says, when there's no grown-ups and you can't go back home because there's no home either.

We're going for a walk, she says.

Why, she says, what are you doing?

So Urban shows them what he's discovered on his recce.

It takes them two hours at Duckling pace, but the coming truth starts to bear down on them about half way there.

It's a brand new end-of-the-world canyon. A rift. Easily a mile deep, and no way of telling how wide or how long. No way across, and to go around could easily become a journey of a whole new magnitude.

From far enough above, looking down, the rift is in the form of a terrified scream. They'll never see it from that angle.

The friends line up along the rim of the canyon, with their backs to the known world. Mirabel squeezes Wolf's hand.

Well, says Duckling. Goodness me. How pretty.

Mirabel doesn't hear him.

Something in the margin of the picture has captured her attention, something in the far corner of the reddening sky.

Duckling observes the angle of her face, the fierce heat of her concentration.

Then Urban notices, then Wolf.

Nobody sees what she sees: but they see her looking.

The language won't come to her lips to tell them about the alien craft.

But instantly it starts to rain.

In fifteen seconds flat the sky has turned all the colours of a child's dream of open heart surgery, and it starts to rain, and the rain is perfectly red.

The friends are soaked to the skin in vermillion rain

and in the corner of the sky, Mirabel watches everything end all over again.

Mirabel's childhood, and all the other childhoods she might have had, catch fire, flare up, and in an instant are gone.

Somebody is singing to us from a very long way away.

There is a great and terrible war in outer space.

Four.

It's clear that Salad is close to death.

Mirabel has laid Salad gently out on the ground, and now she's lying down next to her, face to face, singing a quiet made-up song about some sheep who organize an acrobatics contest on the moon.

She's very poorly, says Wolf. She needs food and water.

But it's a lovely song, says Duckling.

I did say, says Wolf. We did know this would happen if we uprooted her.

Mirabel sits up.

When I'm dying, says Mirabel, please can I have a song. I don't want a sandwich I want a song.

I don't want a roast chicken and roast potatoes and roast peas and roast gravy and roast stupid and roast sky and grass and roast you.

I want a song about sheep and happy bouncing.

Sorrow and rage are scalding Wolf's heart from the inside.

All right, says Mirabel, look, Bear I want you to—

Wolf! says Wolf. Wolf!

I beg your pardon, says Mirabel. Wolf. And Urban. I want you to go to Landmark 22 and wait for us there.

I need to talk to Duckling, says Mirabel.

Human talk, she says.

It is a remark, she knows, of the utmost cruelty.

Urban gently picks up Wolf in his jaws and off they trot to Landmark 22. For days, Wolf has been longing to be properly held. This is not quite it. But it's not nothing.

For a long time, they watch Urban walk away, and then Mirabel's gaze settles on Duckling's squiffy leg. It doesn't feel wrong that she's staring.

Don't be scared, says Duckling.

I'm not, says Mirabel.

No I can see that you're not, says Duckling.

We can't let Salad die, says Mirabel.

Of course we can't, says Duckling. What do you propose?

In my bag, says Mirabel, there's a pink very sharp kitchen knife, and some plasters with *Frozen* on them which is not my favourite film any more.

I think there's still one last Chewit left, too, she says. If you're hungry.

Gently she picks up Salad and holds the limp flower against her forearm.

Don't be scared, says Mirabel.

I'm not, says Duckling.

No I can see that you're not, says Mirabel.

* * *

28

It takes twenty minutes for Wolf to work out what's bothering him.

Of course he's upset about Mirabel. But that's not it.

Dog carried me here. In his mouth.

No drool. No slobber.

Urban has no real smell and now no spit.

An intense blue butterfly comes for a moment and makes Urban bark.

And in time a worm comes, and Wolf watches it curl around into a loop and pop the tip of its tail into its mouth. And then from all along the segments of its body it somehow gives birth to a dozen tiny little baby worms, all giggling and wriggling in the sunshine. And Wolf laughs at this macabre sight and wakes himself up and there are no worms, and for a moment he misses them like crazy.

When Mirabel and Duckling at last arrive, Duckling with Baheegwing under his arm, it's hard to see exactly what's happened.

Mirabel has made a deep cut in her forearm, maybe two-and-a-half inches long. Into this wound she's inserted the bottom two inches of the bluebell's stem, and the stem is fixed there—and the arm held together—with nine Disney sticking plasters. There's been no water so the arm is very bloody. Her face is streaked with dirty tears, though of course we know that couldn't have happened, because Mirabel does not cry. Evidently Duckling, who affixed the plasters while Mirabel held Salad's stem in place, must have allowed his own tears to fall on her face.

In an effort to save Salad's life, we have grafted her onto Mirabel, says Duckling, seeing that an explanation is in order.

It looks a bit alarming, I admit, he says. But it's fairly standard floriculture.

Time, like endless unresolving fear.

She wanted to come, says Mirabel. We couldn't have left her behind. It would have broken her heart.

A flower doesn't have a heart, says Wolf.

You don't have a heart, says Mirabel. You have a broken squeaker which is no good to anyone.

Wolf feels pulverised with anger. He wishes he were dead. He wishes he could heal her beautiful arm with a magic kiss.

He wishes for the butterfly to come back.

Mirabel is suddenly sick on the ground. There's not very much but it's a very intense colour and it comes up very painfully.

Duckling ushers her to a small patch of scrub grass where she can lie down. He takes off his jacket and lies it over her.

Wolf, says Urban.

I wish to object, says Wolf. His voice is shaking as though he might be on the edge of tears, although his body does not contain such a mechanism. A bear that can cry costs at least another £30, in a world where such things still exist at all.

I wish to object in the strongest possible terms, he says, about the way that this story is being written.

I cannot see the point in writing such unnecessary harm, he says.

I really think the writer must now stop.

I honestly think the writer must be mentally ill.

Sssh, says Urban.

Sssh.

Don't wake him.

* * *

Severe night. Mirabel comes to. All of the others are asleep.

In her dreams, the pain in her arm has been, successively, red ants, a shark bite, a television screen, dragon fire, a place for charging your phone. Finally it's black and boiling tar, and she's whispering Help! as she wakes.

Salad is still attached to her arm. Has even perked up a little bit, perhaps.

Duckling is spreadeagled by the last of the campfire. Mirabel wants to give him his coat back.

She sits cross-legged by the head end of Duckling. At what she can't possibly know is 3am exactly, he says out loud, quite clearly: Dinosaur.

Mirabel puts her finger to his lips.

No dinosaur, she says. They're all extinct. Just like us.

There's nothing to wake up for, she says, kindly.

Her eye is caught by a single silverfish climbing out of Duckling's head wound.

She lets the silverfish climb onto her fingerpad, and it looks around for the exit for a bit. Then she helps it find the ground.

She looks at Duckling's head wound and she can't help wanting to know.

Slowly, with intense care, she puts her finger inside the wound, pushes gently until she feels a surface pushing back.

Closing her eyes, dimly inside her mind she sees a room, a picture of a room, in almost black and white, but there's brown and red and purple, and there's candlelight, and gold pictureframes.

The room is a bar. A crowded bar in a European city. Mirabel, who has never been inside a bar, or to Europe, nonetheless sees that it is a crowded room. The door is locked. People drinking grown-up drinks.

Duckling is dreaming, and his dream is in her head.

There is piano music. Adult laughter. A frightening old man with a white moustache. A younger man dressed as a tall blonde woman with a rudely lipsticked mouth.

Someone is sitting in Mirabel's lap. In Duckling's lap. Their lap.

A young man with a bare elegant neck.

Duckling has his arm around the young man in his lap. Young man isn't quite right, is it. Boy.

Duckling leans to kiss the boy. Kisses the boy. The boy kisses back.

Mirabel's first kiss.

She wonders at how old the boy is. Seventeen.

The boy is laughing. It was a pretty good kiss.

Sixteen.

Trying to look away, at the paintings on the wall, the chandelier, the words on the blackboard in an unfamiliar language, Mirabel counts slowly backwards from sixteen, until the age of the boy feels true.

She holds the eventual number in her mind. It's bright, like a poison flower.

She wants to go home.

There are no homes.

She can feel it: someone is eating the flower.

* * *

The next time Mirabel wakes, she is looking at the sky.

Sleepyhead, says Urban.

It's bright white day. A red kite is tracing anonymous signatures far above her head.

Lovely dog, says Mirabel softly.

Listen, he says. We need to take this slowly.

She doesn't know what he means, until she does.

Duckling has had his head smashed in. He's still lying in the same splayed position as before, but his face is distorted beyond all possible faceness, and blood and brain and bits of bone form a wide vague halo all around the place of his head.

Mirabel's breathing feels like lifting a heavy weight and putting it down again, over and over.

Looks like someone dropped a rock on him from a great height, says Urban.

And without hesitation or remorse: Baheegwing, says Baheegwing.

Soon it's time. Mirabel covers Duckling's ruined head with his jacket, and kisses the hem of his sleeve. She gathers a dozen small stones and makes a little cairn.

She says a few words.

She says: I didn't know Officer Duckling very well and I can't remember his real name. But he was very brave. Even when he was crying. And he was very kind.

It's a shame he wasn't a grown-up, she says. It's sad when people die before they're grown-ups.

He let me have the last Chewit.

It doesn't sound like much but it wasn't just like the last Chewit in the pack. It was like The Last Chewit On Earth.

I want to sing a song but I can only think of sheep on the moon one or All Things Bright And Beautiful. And out of all the things in All Things Bright And Beautiful, there's really not much left. It would mostly be humming.

Well. Thank you for your service, Duckling. Goodbye.

And with that, Mirabel sits down, and she peels the *Frozen* plasters off her arm. There's redness and swelling all down the forearm and the cut starts to bleed again as she pulls the plasters away. It's super interesting.

She takes out the slender corpse of Salad, and places it tenderly on Duckling's chest.

Then with all her might she tears a long strip from his ragged trouser leg and wraps it tight around her arm.

There, she says.

And now the next part of the important things.

She picks up Baheegwing and carries him to the edge of the canyon.

You are sentenced to death, she says. Do you have anything you want to say about that?

Baheegwing is silent. The universe is silent.

Well goodbye then, says Mirabel, and she swings her arms, and lets him go, and he's gone. They don't even hear him land.

It's Wolf who sees what's been lying underneath Baheegwing all this time. It glints in the big light.

Urban doesn't see. He's been watching the kite overhead.

Mirabel sees, and picks it up.

It's the right half of a broken nametag.

And on it is the word: MYTH.

* * *

The silence of the great new desert, relentlessly multiplying itself by itself.

White sunlight, like shattered expensive glass.

Wolf says to Mirabel: I want to tell you something you already know.

I've never seen you pet him.

I don't think you've ever petted him.

I think he's the only dog you've ever met and not petted them.

Why's that?

Poor Mirabel.

Wolf has sent Urban off to look for anything they can use to make a better bandage for Mirabel's arm.

Surely Urban knows he's been sent away so that this conversation can be had in private.

We've never talked about his eyes, says Wolf.

I thought they were just trendy, says Mirabel.

A raisin-sized fly comes and goes.

I know you don't like me very much any more, says Wolf, but can I tell you what I think has happened?

Mirabel says nothing. It isn't that she doesn't like him. It's more complicated than that.

It sometimes happens . . . , says Wolf.

. . . that an animal—a dog or a fox or a kangaroo—

I know what an animal is, says Mirabel. Thank you so much.

You don't have the first idea, thinks Wolf, but he doesn't say.

It sometimes happens, he says, that an animal somehow dies

and

but

for whatever reason

they don't know they've died.

And so they stick around.

They don't know.

They have no authentic smell and their name becomes distorted
and you can't pet them because they are not quite present to your
hand.

What do we do? says Mirabel.

When he comes back, says Wolf, we have to tell him to go home.

And we have to be united and persistent and we have to keep
saying it until he goes.

Mirabel nods.

She says Wolf don't ever leave me.

Of course not, he says.

Can we at least have a farewell party for Urban? she says.

Urban comes back, with nothing for the wound.

I'm sorry, he says. I did everything I could.

We know, says Wolf. Thank you, Urban.

Urban Myth, says Urban, bitterly.

Urban Legend, says Wolf.

Thank you Wolf, says Urban. And then he says: Miss?

A human is such a trapped thing, thinks Urban. So trapped inside itself.

Go home Urban, says Mirabel.

Urban is still for a few moments, and then he tilts his head to one side a little, like a famous dog listening to music.

Go home, she says.

And his head straightens and he is absolutely still.

Go home, Urban, she says. Go home. Go home.

Go home, she says. Please, she says.

She feels quite clearly for a moment that she'd rather put her hands round his throat and strangle him to death.

Now she understands why some powerful men can't stand being looked at by another species.

Mirabel goes over and picks up the twelve small stones of Duckling's tiny cairn and cradles them in her hands.

Mirabel and Urban look at each other, and the gap between them in this moment is the worst, most beautiful rift on earth.

Go home, she says, and she throws a stone at his head.

It misses by a mile, but that doesn't matter.

Go home go home go home, she says, pelting Urban with
stones, go home, go home

and it seems to Wolf that though Urban is quite still, it's working,
he's starting to go.

Close your eyes, he tells Mirabel.

And she closes her eyes and throws the rest of the stones one by
one and shouts Go home, go home, I'm begging you, please, go
home

and when she opens her eyes, all she can see is the faintest
outline of Urban, chalk dust and heat haze, the vague shape of
his dear head, a scribble of atoms, nothing really

and she blinks on purpose

and then he's gone.

He's completely gone.

Nothing remains.

He's gone, says Wolf.

Yes I know, says Mirabel.

I can see, she says.

Good dog.

Five.

Landmark 29—the last and grandest—comes disguised as a mirage, shining and quavering on the far side of an incomprehensible distance.

It looks like exactly the sort of promise that Mirabel has resolved never to trust again. But it's not like they've got anything else to walk towards.

They're almost at the entrance before they'll allow themselves to believe what they know. It's real. It's a real building.

The big sign across the front of the mall is no longer illuminated, and that jaunty angle might not be intentional, but they can still read the giant words: THE ESMERELDA CENTRE.

And down at ground level, when Mirabel walks towards the big glass doors, they still open inwards automatically, and a big sign says 'Welcome!' in fake handwriting.

For two hours it's been buzzing in the back of Mirabel's mind that if this building were real, it might have food, and water, and shelter, and a chocolate fountain, and medical supplies.

But what makes her feel overwhelmed in the end is the music that's coming over the tannoy. Just the blandest muzak, but it's so rich to her ears that she instantly bends over and starts to retch.

In the ladies toilet, the mirror is shattered and smeared with what looks like blackberries, and the water from the taps is a thick grudging ooze of cardigan beige, and half way up the wall is a strange spontaneous anus out of which baby spiders are spilling profusely. Mirabel's reflection in the mirror is the face of a crash test dummy who's died eight times a day for forty days in a whole playlist of industrial accidents.

Wolf is waiting for her in the main atrium.

Where to, madam? he says. There's a Kingdom of Sweets on the first floor, look.

Or there's a Primark if you fancy a sunhat.

Let's just walk around, says Mirabel.

All the plants are fake. In fact they're less like real plants than no plants would have been.

There is a waffle stall, but even the smell makes Mirabel feel sick again. It's so sweet and so disgusting. She feels like she wants to eat cress. There was blotting paper on the windowsill at home with cress growing on it. And for a moment she mourns for the cress more than she's ever mourned for her parents, or even for Duckling.

This must be where they all came when the world ended, thinks Mirabel, as she wanders the chromium streets of the abandoned mall. Maybe they all ascended into heaven and left her behind.

Everything in John Lewis is sleeping neatly folded. Takes more than armageddon to disturb those polo shirts.

All the glasses in the window of Vision Express look silently on as Mirabel and Wolf dance past.

And then Mirabel stops outside a branch of Claire's Accessories.

CLOSING DOWN, says a notice in the window.

That's quite the understatement, says Wolf.

Mirabel presses her nose up to the window. The lights are off but she can just make out the contents of the shop.

Unicorn pendants and holographic owls on bracelets and Doug the Pug in a Hawaiian shirt and headbands with stars on and cat ears and princess tiaras and rainbow pens and panda sleep masks and unicorn bath bombs and gold pearl flower crowns and sequinned fascinators and rainbow dreamcatchers and Doug the Pug in a panda onesie and rainbow unicorns and rainbow infinity pendants and a plushy blue winged horse named Emmeline.

Very painstakingly, Mirabel counts all the things and there are exactly a million.

Claire, she says.

Claire.

I think Claire's gone, says Wolf.

I know, says Mirabel.

I hope she's OK without all her shit.

They walk around some more, though Wolf keeps offering nap time, he can see how totally exhausted she is. The shops all start to blend into a multicoloured grey. Barely various qualities of light. The music just keeps coming out endlessly like gradually fading suicide notes from an unattended photocopier.

On the far wall Wolf sees an illuminated arrow, and a silhouette of a little girl and a teddy bear next to it. EMERGENCY EXIT, it says.

Come on, says Wolf.

For the first time he's aware that this shopping mall has clouds. It's so big it has its own weather.

They follow the emergency exit signs, past a soft play area that looks untouched, and a champagne bar and a grand piano; through a plastic jungle and past a diorama of half-size dinosaurs; past pinball machines and a decommissioned Challenger tank.

And they turn a corner, and there is a single escalator, going up.

And it goes up and up, into the clouds and beyond.

No twin escalator coming down.

And it says: EMERGENCY EXIT.

And underneath that, it says: Face direction of travel. Dogs must be carried.

We haven't got a dog, says Wolf. What shall we do?

That's an old joke, says Mirabel. But I love you.

I thought there'd be more jokes along the way, didn't you?, says Wolf.

Well, says Mirabel, but the world died.

Mirabel, says Wolf.

Yes well I'm going to go now, says Mirabel.

You don't need me any more, says Wolf.

Oh, she says. No but I do think it's time for us to part. She says: I think you need to live a wolf life now.

Possibly, says Wolf. I'm not sure a wolf life has a lot of hugs.

Well, says Mirabel. Living the right life is better than hugs.

43

And then she hugs him anyway. And he knows this hug is his work ending.

And then she sets him down.

Mirabel, he says.

But she's already stepped backwards onto the bottom step of the escalator, and she's smiling at him in a way that she hasn't since the end of the previous world.

Face direction of travel! says Wolf, pointing at the sign.

I am, says Mirabel, cheerfully, looking at Wolf as she starts to ascend.

I am facing in the direction of everything I know.

But I am travelling backwards upwards in the direction of what I don't know. Yet.

I'm facing in the direction of high fidelity.

But I am travelling backwards in the direction of irresistible progress.

I am travelling backwards towards overdue reparation.

Towards pre-vandalised schools and liberated zoos.

I'm facing in the direction of constancy and simulated moderation.

But I'm travelling backwards upwards towards a broken codex of the law of love.

I'm facing in the direction of valour and intimacy and their steadfast embodiment by the very best of plush.

44

But I am travelling upwards towards the protections afforded by weaponised sound.

I am travelling backwards towards pragmatic nonideological terrorism and sugarfree variants of energy drinks.

I am travelling towards protocols invented by blind robots with tantalum olfactory receptors.

I'm facing in the direction of trust and its reckless and constant obliteration.

I am travelling backwards towards observable epidemics of chronic lung disease among service industry workers in strange communities.

I'm travelling upwards towards endless circular conversations propelled by recreational anxiolytics.

Towards astronaut food being fed to cattle and vending machines that dispense actual human excrement.

I'm facing in the direction of functional language being humiliated by leering paparazzi hired by the super-rich.

I'm travelling towards mouthwash that knows what I'm thinking, and caramel printed guns that the Dalai Lama says are a superfood.

I'm facing in the direction of hawthorn woods chaotically smattered with afterbirth.

I'm travelling backwards towards free-at-the-point-of-access mainstream heterosexual pornography that is nothing but punching and headbutting.

Travelling upwards towards goldfinches that have been genetically modified to harvest data and communicate with mother-drones.

Backwards and upwards until my head is in the clouds—

And slowly Mirabel vanishes into the crowd of clouds at the top of the Esmerelda Centre, and is lost to the vision of Wolf, with his one milky eye and his untilting head and no appreciable neck.

But he fancies he can hear her still describing her own disappearance in the most accurate detail, and he listens for as long as he can hear.

I am facing in the direction of raggedy half-naked youths running for their lives in municipal forests and sacrificing the white of their trainers.

But I am travelling upwards towards their opposite, and the unwavering diagrams of that opposite and their labelling in a font called All-Out Total Helvetica.

Backwards into a dream of a smart fluid that is introduced into the lymphatic system of every newborn when the payment clears.

Backwards and upwards into the election pledge of a habitable thermopause that has already learned to forgive me.

Backwards and upwards into the black finality of a broken man's imagination.

Backwards and upwards into the black milk.

Backwards and upwards into the bruise.

The wound of my own arm

and the wound's wound

Coda.

CHRIS is suddenly out in front again, back in his white shirt and dark suit from the top of the show. He takes a vocal mic from a stand, like a stand-up. The sound level feels a bit too high, the quality a bit harsh.

Dr Garabedian ends his shift with a long piss. Like a *long* piss, like where's all this coming from, like am I actually hollow inside. It's all good. The end of the day, to be undisturbed, just alone in a small room holding your penis. Don't forget to pick up a bottle of Tanqueray on the way home. Why does holding your penis remind you of gin. Long day. Slightly too cursory hand wash, quick rubbish dry. Back out into the corridor, along to the consulting room where he's been working today. Jacket. Briefcase. Can't be arsed to switch off the lights. Phone doesn't even ring. Smashing it. Says good night to Alma. Good night Dr Garabedian, says Alma. That mouth. Holy moly. Good night to Jeremy. Squash next Wednesday yeah. Prick. Just puts his head round to say good night to Paul and Molly. Good night Dr Garabedian, says Molly. Paul doesn't acknowledge him. Fair enough. They're exhausted. The time they've spent at Mirabel's bedside and it's not until you've worked for a while with juvenile coma patients and their families that you properly hear how vigil and vigilance are the same word, like a vigil's more than just not going home. Like some Russian teenage hacker took your kid and encrypted them for no ransom. They're going to have to have a very difficult conversation in a day or two at the outside. But they don't know that and they don't have to yet, except maybe Paul already does. He might already be there, in hell or whatever. There's a kid in the lift, maybe six or seven, fucking screaming at the top of his voice like he thinks they're going down in the lift to the car park where he's going to be shot in the head by the mob or something. Lift doors open, out through the lobby past the Costa and the Smiths through the automatic doors into the car park. Kid's still screaming but nobody seems to want to execute Dr Garabedian. More luck than judgement. Staff car park round the side under the awning. Doors bipbip open. Jacket and briefcase on the back seat. Nearly empty Burger King XL Diet Coke still in the cup holder from a week ago. Seatbelt, ignition. Never quite sure that a bomb won't go off. Later than he thought. Fuck. Radio on.

Loud intense minimal techno starts to blast out of the car radio.

Fuck. Passport renewal. Come on bro get it together. Tonight tonight tonight. Bottle of Tanqueray, passport renewal. Mock the Week. Still fucking tense from Geraldine talking about her yacht. Her yacht. Geraldine's yacht. That's a weird word, how did that happen? Y-A-C-H-T, *yacht*. You know it's / Yacht! / it's amazing how far you can get without actually paying attention to the road, to the driving, to the traffic lights. Not ignoring, just it's all on auto. Alma's a good name for a parrot. Bright red one. But don't get a parrot. You're like, let's get a parrot, but after a while, aren't you just going, there's a parrot in my house. Like a joke. Like, waiter, there's a parrot in my house. Come to think of it, there's a waiter in my house. It's easier to just move house, just abandon your house, let the waiter and the parrot have the house, go and live on a longboat. A narrowboat. What's the difference between a narrowboat and a longboat? See that's supposedly a relaxing way of life but what if you're awake at 2am going what's the difference between a narrowboat and a longboat. Get to 45 and you don't know shit anymore. Fuck me Garabedian you smell like hospital. When does a smell become a stench? Hospital gets under your skin. Like a secret. Hospital knows where you live. It knows how you're sleeping. Fuck off Hospital. Like there's no such thing as a wideboat, right? Hot Cheetos. Passport renewal.

Bottle of Tanqueray, bottle of decent tonic, passport renewal tonight without fail, Flamin' Hot Twisted Cheetos. Mirabel dies in a part of his head but that's him doing that, that's not, that's him doing that. Partly she reminds him of that girl, that ghost of that girl, that documentary, years ago now, very different circumstances. Different girls' faces just you know. It's all good. And then in the corner of the widescreen windscreen, coming round the roundabout, there's a flying saucer in the top right, glowing red and green, the same colours as a downtown chicken shop, Chick Lit or Colonel Fernandos, and the burning quiet of the distance of the UFO, the childish outline, amateurish really. No one is even filming it with their phone. Everyone thinks it's someone else's hallucination. Dr Garabedian flashes back for a moment to when his paternal grandmother would make him say his prayers before bed when he was five or six and he secretly prayed to Space Invaders. That guest bedroom, he's thinking about, the codes in those curtains, the optical illusions of a whole childhood, and then he's turning into his road, how did that happen, everything on auto, and no / fuck / gin and no tonic and no whatever, the other thing. Another night of this kind of night. He opens the front door and takes off his shoes, leaves them with the shoes. He says hi to Trish who is on the phone and goes straight upstairs to check in on his girls. And there they are in their bunk beds and he's home too late again to kiss them good night but they understand and it's great they understand and it's good to understand. And he's out of their bedroom again and walking away from the thing that keeps being there, walking down the landing away from it, down the landing to the bathroom, to splash cold water on his face, and then away from it again, and back down the stairs, and he calls out to Trish, FORGOT THE GIN, he says, WHAT A WALLY, he says, and he's back outside, walking away from the thing, which is this, we might as well name this. He wonders who he is in their dreams, his girls, what dreams of him they will never have, he wonders

49

what is actually known about his girls, and he has not put any
shoes on and it seems that he is walking to the offie, no shoes
no wallet, he's walking away from the thing, the thing is he loves
them so much, his girls, he'd die for his girls, like that, he's almost
sorry he probably won't, and a greyhound trots on its own down
the pavement towards him, past him, and he's walking away from
the thing which is still not said, which is this: that he loves them
with all his heart, and that's the reason he pretends not to know
that there's a glitch

                        a half-second glitch that he feels in
his nervous system right before he knows that he loves them
where he sees them sleeping and he hates them. He feels in his
heart that he hates his little daughters, sleeping in their bunk
beds, he knows that he hates them for literally half a second
before he loves them. And he's out on the pavement and he
loves his girls so much and another greyhound trots on its own
down the pavement towards him, past him, weird, and no way
of paying for the gin or the tonic, no shoes on his feet, and he
wants you to know how much he hates them, his daughters,
they're six and three, they're utterly blameless, and he hates
them so much, for not more than half a second before he loves
them, and there was no such glitch, and two more greyhounds
trot together down the pavement towards him, what the fuck is
up with these greyhounds, and he kneels and intercepts one of
the greyhounds and the other trots on, and he's kneeling on the
pavement, this greyhound staring, and the greyhound knows
about the glitch, but there is no such glitch, this is absolutely
outrageous, and he's holding this greyhound's head in his hands,
saying AREN'T YOU? to the greyhound, saying AREN'T YOU,
CUNT?, and he grips the greyhound's head in his hands and for
a moment it looks like he's sinking towards the dog and towards
the ground like he's going in for a cuddle, and then he opens his
mouth over the dog's head and he bites down

50

doctor biting the greyhound's head
and the greyhound's wigging out and the doctor holding the
greyhound's body like a wrestling move and he bites down
harder into the dog's head until he thinks his teeth have touched
skull and he's biting and there is no such glitch and there is blood
and stink and it's very frank and the dog is shouting for help
and nobody is coming and nobody and nobody is here and the
flying saucer was not real or it was real then and not now and the
doctor is biting the greyhound's head and death is riding riding
and the rain will be blood and he absolutely fucking loves his
girls and the family holiday and the

doctor biting the greyhound's head

doctor biting the greyhound's head

doctor biting the greyhound's head

doctor biting the greyhound's head

doctor biting the greyhound's head

DOCTOR BITING THE GREYHOUND'S HEAD

DOCTOR BITING THE GREYHOUND'S HEAD

DOCTOR BITING THE GREYHOUND'S HEAD

DOCTOR BITING THE GREYHOUND'S HEAD

DOCTOR BITING THE GREYHOUND'S HEAD

DOCTOR BITING THE GREYHOUND'S HEAD

This is repeated, with limited variations maybe, for as long as anyone can bear it.

At some point the techno track ends.

And on we go, no music, no sound other than these words in a bare room.

And on.

And then at the point when it just can't be said any more:

OK, good.

Blackout.